CARS AND PEOPLE

CARS AND PEOPLE

Pissing at 60 miles
an hour

●

Anthony Douglas Ziegler

Writers Advantage
New York   Lincoln   Shanghai

Cars and People
Pissing at 60 Miles an Hour

Writers Advantage
an imprint of iUniverse, Inc.

For information address:
iUniverse
2021 Pine Lake Road, Suite 100
Lincoln, NE 68512
www.iuniverse.com

ISBN: 0-595-25917-0 (Pbk)
ISBN: 0-595-65432-0 (Cloth)

Printed in the United States of America

Never hold any man to a standard of ethics of which you are incapable of reaching.

Joe Fuken Blow

Contents

Silence

If silence were the name of a kitten, I would have heard her during my birth, coughing up hairballs within the clotting sunrise. She would've become my birthday. I would've passed like breath through fresh whiskers. I would've breathed that day.

Las Vegas

Early morning Vegas purred, resurrecting people chasing work schedules. We passed each other through exhaust tail syrup, sipping cappuccino, lips pursed in lament of our childhood; recalling whiskey straight; twelve years old behind the boat shed next door neighbor nude and goose-bumped between hay scratches screaming, "Fuck me!"

This was the beginning of the decline our parents noticed in us. We wore our favorite Sunday school outfits, skipping through the parking lot under praise of fathers and gods. Everything happened last week, last year, and as far back as adolescence. It all happened in the morning in a little town dressed an awful lot like a showgirl.

Embalming Fluid

There's something about the Nevada dawn that made breakfast in Vegas reek of her death. The sun bleakly cut across desertscapes to dance through Dolly's diner window and a stale mug of coffee until it came to rest in his eye. He could see her reflection in the spoon he used to mix morning and blackness, like an orgy of embalming fluid and her touch. "I'm still in love," he thought. "Too bad she's dead."

Dead

He would have enjoyed her dead. At least he enjoyed entertaining the idea that she was dead. She wasn't, obviously.

Though beautiful alive, she would have been just as alluring dead. In her sleep she managed to move gracefully. Sleep and death are quite similar. She could star in her own *Ballet de Mort*, choreographed entirely by her, asleep.

Breakfast

It's incredible what a man thinks about during breakfast.

His eggs were runny and she wasn't really dead. He had to think of her as being dead. Death would make his leaving a bit more comfortable.

Buffet

For much of the dawn she'd been awake, lying in her hair, weeping. While he thought she was asleep, she was awake. When he pulled his arm from her nest of brown hair, she was awake. She was awake during every step he took from the bed and awake in the muted hinges of the door when it closed.

Brown hair as thin as hers wakes easily, beginning the day with the sun and morning-city-traffic-breath that smells like a 7-11 coffee and carbon monoxide buffet. It's not unusual for hair as brown as hers to do such things. It happens often in most U.S. cities, and Las Vegas is no exception, though some parts of Caliente are.

7:46 a.m. downtown on the Strip Postcard

Even the cafe windows are too cold to touch, he thought, pressing his cheeks against their surfaces to examine the clouds. The early sun shakes its blonde hair through the morning horizon, pushing sky apart like the dance floor of a thousand mad Indians, drinking with their horses and heroes and digging the whole retro Southern Nevada Indian scene.

Dawn dances best in the desert city. He'd been through America, watching and moving with the dawn, jerking to tarnished brass bells throughout his life. There are no postcards capable of challenging the taste of 7:46 a.m. downtown on the strip.

Green Valley Parkway

I grew up here; tangled in the nape of the mountain. Green Valley Parkway runs from one end of Vegas to the other, and from one end of my childhood up to the air of today.

Eighteen and stoned on Carson Street. Standing below City Hall and a statue of someone's father staring left over his shoulder. I swear that statue looked at me. He stood there, smiling, half-cognitive, turned his head around and winked.

Eleven years, couple hundred phone calls, sixty-one jobs, twenty-five more pounds and eight cars later the street's the same. This is why I live here; dry night sky blooming; dusk splash; washing long hair in its clean, cool breath. Breathe in silence.

Smoker

Everyone's a smoker when they're among friends. They smoke or they have smoked. They stand around in clouds thickening behind their heads and chat about smoking and quitting.

Everyone's a quitter when they're among friends. They share tories of winning and losing and sometimes quitting. They smile between stories when they should be crying. There are few tears shed while they smile.

They wait for the drive home after work. That's when they cry. It's easy to do. Many of them have been doing this for years. Some, for just a few days. Green peas learn quickly. There are enough cigarettes to go around and the morning is friendly. Besides, the world loves friendly smokers who quit. It's an obsession and men can be easily obsessed when they're bored.

Boring

There are many thinks to thing about when you're in the car business.

The car business is boring. Time waits for us to carve its face from ice. It's free time and we kill it with thoughts of a dead friend we haven't seen since fifth grade. It's exciting the first time we answer the phone. It's exciting until we realize that our friend has changed. Our friend has changed in every way. He's grown up and away from us and we've moved away from him. He's grown and died. He's dead and now he's going away from us. He's changing. He's no longer the friend he used to be before we went and left the neighborhood and before he went and left the world. Death is boring, like the car business.

He

He's getting old. His wife notices this from the bathroom of their motor home when she cranes her neck. He drives lazily out of the driveway they raised two kids in, racing toward retirement.

She can see a few drops of his urine at her feet. His sight has been affected with the movement of his death. She doesn't slow him down. There is no reason for him to drive cautiously. He can't die any sooner.

Music responds to her senses and no tears dry mixed in his urine. It's the Beatles on the radio for the thirtieth year in a row. She's happy to watch him enjoying his first few minutes of retirement while she listens, continuing her pissing at sixty miles an hour.

Recreational Vehicular Manslaughter

They sold their house and bought an RV to drive them to their graves. Twenty-four years as a car salesman and 282,112 cigarettes later he lights his first retirement smoke. He'll barely have time to enjoy it before stopping for gas. His life is no different.

Fifty-six; old for a smoker. No male in his family lived much longer than fifty-six. They all smoked and ate and died of heart disease. He's retired now. Maybe he'll quit tomorrow.

Cocaine

"Damnit!"

It's 7:46 a.m. on a Wednesday, on the last day of November. These are the only facts Scott's sure of. The only true facts, other than the fact that it's a minute after he should be at work. And the fact that his glass pipe is somewhere on the far side of his bare living room. The far side of his bare world. A world away from his bare ass.

He's pissed. It's normal to be this way when you can't find your coke. It happens every day; people kept from their stash, pissed, cursing, and nude.

"Damnit!"

Furniture

He was a salesman. He's always been very sales oriented.

During Scott's second grade summer vacation his step-father told him to get rid of a pick-up full of rocks that had been left in his backyard. Every day he painted a wagon full gold and silver on one side only and walked through Salinas selling them to his hundred-year-old neighbors for as much as ten bucks a set. By July the backyard was empty and he had $932.

Scott couldn't save money. He'd always been very loose with his cash. If he had saved his money then he wouldn't have had to sell his furniture.

Empty Dead Room

Nothing about Scott's room is familiar. It has no useful space and no positive attribute. There have never been any Tupperware parties, bridge tournaments, Amway conventions, fondue rituals, disco orgies or AA meetings held there. In no way does his room remind him of his mother's place except for the wall-to-wall avocado shag carpet. He has no furniture. It's only an empty, dead room.

<u>Drowning</u>

Anne had been lying in a puddle of her weeping brown hair that usually fell off her shoulders when she was sitting up in bed. She was lying down now, barely awake and drowning in a puddle of her hair while she watched Don snore.

Sometimes Don slept without breathing. She could never tell if he was breathing. Sometimes she wished that Don would stop snoring. Sometimes she wished that he would stop breathing. Usually he did both for brief periods of time.

Sleeping and Crying

Don slept.
Anne cried.

Bed Fart

He'd been sleeping since he returned from his early morning drunkenness, stumbling through the bedroom with one leg out of his pants and the other caught at the ankle.

Anne didn't like his drinking. Not because he looked like an idiot trying to navigate his ass to bed and not because of the time she was left alone while he drank. She enjoyed both of these side effects that came with his drinking. She didn't like the beer farts. She hated the beer farts. Beer and farts and Anne didn't mix well.

Don was a beer-drinking, beer-farting champion of champions. If there had been an Olympic event centered around beer farting Don would have held the world's record for the duration of their relationship. Don loved the smell of a good beer fart. Anne didn't.

Anne thought it a miracle that he made it to bed that evening. He'd step and stop and sway and fart and giggle and fall. She enjoyed his falling and would often compare it to the ending credits in her mind. They didn't own a T.V.

He's Dead Looking

He saw himself crawling across the room to his death. It's easy to do when you're late for work and crawling across the floor looking for a crumb of cocaine. He saw himself dead, and there's nothing he thinks of any more except his death.

Nobody cares. He has no furniture to sell and no money to divide among the family he doesn't have. It was a quick book he crawled in. That's all.

The Sex Life of Don & Anne

<u>2:00 a.m.</u>

Step.
Stop.
Sway…
thwppp!
Giggle.
Fall.

Mother

His mother bought her carpet at a remnant sale in the parking lot of a giant artichoke. All of the artichoke's windows were busted out, covering the toes of Castroville. It was an artichoke where he began life in love with the flavor of mayonnaise. They sell carpet and fruit and blow jobs and artichokes. That's all there is to sell in Castroville.

When he closed his eyes he found the dampness of dust. It's a dampness only found in pictures that line the walls of every empty, dead room there has ever been. The pictures are black and white photographs of small children running from a school bus on fire.

His mother used to walk him to the bus stop.

They Didn't Own a T.V.

Anne had a T.V. when she first met Don. They used to sit up at night watching re-runs of "The Honeymooners" and "I Love Lucy."

Later in their relationship, Don would sleep with occasional beer farts that toasted Anne's stomach.

This

There is something about all of this, so familiar that he wouldn't need to breath his name without you agreeing you must have met at least once before. He saw himself as a dead car salesman who used to be a trusting child.

It's between here and there; beneath the shadows of two friends on their phones, leaning toward one another. It's popcorn sticking to our pants during a matinee; salty butter drying under fingernails. A first kiss in the back of the theater, heart racing, dizzy light-headed smiling temple to temple, exhausted; erection pressing breast to blue jean wet like flannel teenager sheets spinning around in the rinse cycle while parents snore. It's between friends.

This is who he used to be. This is who he has become. There is little difference between the two. Now there is no reason to continue to compare and no reason to write of this again. The butter is dry.

More on the Sex Life of Don & Anne

Don slept.
Anne cried.

She never Woke Up

He remembers moving the yellow comforter over her like an arm belonging to her father. It draped her affectionately, mixing with her long brown hair, webbed across her face, eroding her bass fish mouth into the pillow he'd pulled his hand out from under.

She never woke up.

He almost thought her cold, waiting for the morgue to pack her away in a three-ply trash bag commercial. She slept like flowers grown in ice and all the while he meant to smell her before he left. He didn't. He was sure that had he tried he wouldn't have paid much attention to the fragrance he knew as her.

Awake

Don woke earlier than usual.

Anne had her back to him, pretending to sleep.

Don's breathing quieted and his eyes lifted a yellow, duck-crafted comforter, like a wave for him to roll out from under its currents.

Anne lay there with her eyes closed, crying. Though she never opened her eyes while he dressed, her eyes never drowned in themselves. They were shallow tears that managed to find their way into the crack of her forearm resting under her cheek.

She cried.

Her hair wept.

He left.

She opened her eyes.

7:47 a.m.

Anne should be moving her pelvis through the bed attempting to find him.

It's been two hours since Don left her forever.

Anne opened her eyes.

As a rule of thumb, minimum wage is $4.25

Ruby used to say, "Son, you'll never get anywhere in this world by lying, cheating, or stealing." She's his mother. She should know.

She has worked for a major department store since she was nineteen. Thirty something years and now she's an assistant manager, making $7.35 an hour.

If he were at work he'd get his final check today. He sold sixteen cars in twenty-two days knowing as much as a mechanical chicken does about automobiles. After deductions his check reads, "Two thousand, Four-hundred, and Eighty dollars and nine cents."

Mother knows best.

Cars & People

Mr. Empire stands to his shoulder, when his shoulder gets to work. He's 5'1" with eyes that float in Crown Royal while his teeth shatter melting ice, yellow and gum less.

It's a peculiar business he's in. Cars. A business about the economy and people.

"It's just fucking cars and people. That's all it is. It's cars and fucking people. You just gotta know how to put the two together."

At the Empire lot this phrase haunts everybody's head under midnight sweat and hangover fragrances; a mixture of embalming fluid and baby laxative.

Re-Runs

Their sex life wasn't always the way it was when Don left Anne. Don loved sex when they first met. Anne loved T.V. when they first met.

Don stayed up late, watching T.V. with Anne hoping they could have sex afterwards. Sometimes they did. Frequently they didn't.

"Honey," Don would moan.

"Get the light," Anne would reply.

Click

"Honey?"

"Yeah."

"I love you." He always said 'I love you' because he knew she liked to hear that she was loved.

"Not tonight," She always said 'not tonight' because she knew he liked to beat off in the bathroom.

(Silence)

"Honey? Please." (Tickle. Nudge. Kiss.)

(Silence)

"Tomorrow."

"That's what you said last night."

"Tomorrow. I promise."

It wasn't long after a few weeks of nighttime bed-chat like this that Don decided to throw the T.V. out the bedroom window. Their sex life didn't improve with the T.V. on the front lawn.

Don stopped asking for sex.

Anne noticed.

Nothing

Mr. Empire's car is always clean. The best cars in the world are the ones that he drives and sells. He drives this one like the Statue of Liberty behind a tugboat. It's fresh in the morning. Nobody shops for a car at 7:47 a.m. on a Wednesday, late in November.

Mr. Empire knows this. He drinks knowing this. They watch him mumble, drunken, trying to program them into believing that none of this is true.

"It's the biggest fucking shopping week of the year!"

Every week is the biggest; every day is the final day; it's another sale and there is nothing more important demanding their attention. Nothing. Not the pipe on the floor, the money my friend owes me or the subtle footsteps of angels. Nothing.

Black

"Wanta refill, Baby?" A gum smacking, forty-ish smoker brunette with menstrual red lips hung gravely above him. She seemed too large for the room, eclipsing the fluorescent lighting, covering Don in her shadow. She had waistline breasts half-buried like an economy funeral in a polyester smock.

"What?" Don asked.

"Coffee? Ya want some?"

"Sure." Feeling like a ceramic fart he pushed his cup out from under his chin and watched her pour.

"Ya take her black?"

"Yeah. That's fine," he responded. She smiled, smacking her gum, pulling a kerchief from her pocket. "Waitin' for someone?"

"No. Why do you ask?"

"No reason." She blew her nose, and withdrew her coffee pot to return to the back side of the counter.

Don wiped the edge of his cup with his napkin.

Just Black

He liked his coffee just black. Just black meant no sugar and no cream. No anything that isn't considered a primary root of coffee, for example no mucous.

He wiped the edge of his coffee cup with his napkin.

Lover

Scott was a lover. I want you to know this.

He was a smoker, a car salesman, a liar, and a cocaine addict. He was also a friend, a neighbor, an asshole, a son. All of this is good to know. Over and above all else, Scott was a lover.

Non-Smoker

Scott quit smoking eight days before his birthday.

"Happy Birthday!" she said.

"An ashtray."

"I wanted to get you something you could use."

How was she to know he'd quit smoking? He'd been busy doing his cocaine and getting fired while she was busy with whatever it was that she did with her life. She didn't have a clue.

"Well, I haven't seen you for a while."

"Whose fault is that?" Scott replied without remembering that this is the lady he happened to be sort of in love with, then remembering. "Sorry."

(Sobbing) "That's not very fair."

"Look. It's a nice ashtray. If I were to need an ashtray, this would be the one I'd use. Stop cryin'."

Scott had met her this way; crying. He was standing at the bus stop and she was there standing next to him with a bag of clothes in her arms. "Why are you cryin'?" he'd asked when he met her.

She continued to cry.

"Do you want to talk?"

She continued to cry.

"Look. I'm not one for riding busses. You want to get some coffee? What do you say? Dolly's? My treat."

Still crying, she nodded "Okay" and coffee led to "You should see my place" and "Oh my God! No! No! Yessss!"

He never should have fucked her.

If he hadn't fucked her, she wouldn't be standing in front of him, crying with those tears he'd seen so many times before. If he hadn't fucked her, he wouldn't have "sort of fallen in love" with her. If he hadn't fucked her, he wouldn't have to ask her questions like, "Why don't you leave the bastard?" And he wouldn't have to hear her reply, "I was leaving him when you went and fucked me and made me feel guilty."

If. If. If. Of course, if I had eight arms and lived in Britany Spears' body I'd forget about the sunlight.

"I'm sorry. It's a nice ashtray." Scott spoke softly, lifting her chin to see her puffy red eyes.

"Happy (Sob) Birthday."

<u>He Hated Ashtrays</u>

Scott remembers closing the door behind her, *Click*, listening to her nearly completed crying walk down the hallway.

It wasn't really his birthday. He enjoyed getting gifts and told everyone he met that his birthday was exactly a month away. Most of his relationships didn't last a month. For those that did he was sure to receive some sort of compensation for his endeavors.

"An ashtray."

He hated ashtrays.

Gone

The ceiling of plaster dripping stillness like a sculpture of poverty hung teasingly above Anne. Her hair still soaked the tears she used to drown out the footsteps of the last three years.

They hadn't all been bad years. The first two years were her fondest. Those were the years of touching and snuggling and sex in the kitchen sink and candy eaten from the back pockets of dirty jeans.

Don was gone.

She hadn't moved from bed where she was content staring at the ceiling and crying and dreaming and thinking of past and its finality. She knew he was gone, though. The door didn't click when he left. Doors click when the person leaving is returning at some point. That's the job of the door, to click and let everyone know that it will reopen in a while for that person leaving to return. The door never clicked.

She cried.

Her hair wept.

He left.

(No Click)

She opened her eyes.

Don was gone.

Anne

She opened her eyes for the first time in three years.

Beatles

They want to hold her hand. She too is tracing bumps in the ceiling above her bed. It's late in the sixties and her tye-dye hangs over the nightstand. An 8-track tape player screeches in stereo. Friends are jealous that she lives on the good side of town. She's stoned and doesn't give a shit, busy finding Ringo's face in the textures above her.

Her right hand is too busy to be held. What's left of a joint burns out in her left hand.

She was sixteen once, before his retirement. None of this is happening anymore. She's busy pissing and there is no reason to think of this again.

In November

There are no real car gurus. There are only people like me and Johnny and Don and Scott and Vinny and Bob. There are millions of us and we stand around in small groups sipping coffee, smoking cigarettes, talking about how to fuck or who to fuck or why to fuck.

We stand around at 7:47 a.m. and count heads. We try to remember who works with us and wonder who has quit or been fired or who hasn't shown up at work yet to do either of the two.

It's our job to wonder and we do it with the simple perfection of a sixteen-year-old virgin's frostbit tits. We do it in the cold morning of Las Vegas to see which one of us is missing late in November. We stand up straight and shiver.

Today

Today is no different. Vinny sips and smokes with visions of fish gills under direct sunlight in the hair of morning air over a southern Nevada lakebed. Its a morning opera. Nobody sings.

"How long you been selling?" I asked.

"Fifteen years," he said, letting out a final breath.

"Fifteen years. How much longer will you do it for?"

"Fifteen minutes."

Fifteen Minutes

Vinny believes that fifteen minutes is all that a person can possibly conceive. Everything in life can be scheduled but fifteen minutes is all we know.

We know how we need to be somewhere or get ready to be somewhere or decide not to go somewhere we've been always fifteen minutes before we decide to take action.

It took fifteen minutes to conceive us and fifteen minutes for the pregnancy test to come through. It was a fifteen-minute nail-biter and a fifteen minute phone call with crying and tears that fell and dried on the floor in fifteen minutes before she went to sleep. Fifteen minutes before the door closed behind feet leaving.

I don't necessarily agree with him. Then again, I don't have to. Besides, what would I know about cars?

Still More on the Sex Life of Don & Anne

He began drinking. Drinking was what he was best at and we like to do what we're best at. Don was best at drinking.

Anne would stay home and stare at the space where the T.V. used to be when Don went out. She'd stay home and think about the times she used to say "No!" when their sex life was perfect and she'd wonder what had happened to their perfect sex life. She'd stay home and read *Cosmopolitan* and answer the articles about relationships gone awry and the poor sex lives that are inevitable with these types of relationships. She'd stay home and cry.

Anne would cry, feeling guilty about saying "No!" when she used to watch the T.V. that she couldn't watch anymore unless she went out on the front lawn.

Here, Boy!

"Hey," Don yelled across the cafe.

(No response from the waitress)

"Hey! I'm talking to you."

The waitress had her back to Don. She heard him the first time he yelled and knew he was yelling to get her attention. The cafe was empty with the exception of her, Don and the cook, who had been asleep for the last few hours.

"Excuse me. I'm talking to you."

She looked over her shoulder at Don. "Me? Do you want to talk to me?"

"Of course I want to talk to you. Do you see anybody else here? You heard me. Right?"

"I heard you, son," she replied with eyes doing that thing that women's eyes do when their in absolute bitch state. "I ain't deaf and I ain't your mutt. You want to talk to me. Great. Talk to me, not at me. Start by saying 'excuse me.'"

"Well, I don't know your name. You're not wearing a name badge. I sure the hell don't resemble fucking Nostradamus and I'm not going to say 'Hey waitress.' Is that what you want me to do?"

Silence poured through the cafe as the two of them looked at each other.

"Kat."

"What?"

"Kat. Call me Kat."

"Kat. Do you happen to know when the bus will be here?" he said in his best ego-riddled, condescending voice. This was his favorite voice. He liked using this voice on waitresses, and whatever other women might sit still long enough for him to share it with them.

"Two days." Kat replied in her favorite voice as well. This was the voice she enjoyed using on children, and whatever men would talk to her long enough to remind her of children.

Rock Candy

I forgot about my friend on the way to work. There's too much to see. Though the scenery changes every day, I forget friends and debts due until I'm standing on the pad with a hot cup of watered-down coffee.

During my ride to work I pass a parking lot where people leave their old cars. "For Sale" signs stare out car windows like suffocating abandoned children. The cars wait under street dust while I pass quietly trying not to wake the dead. It's a cemetery and there are no visitors this time of day.

Epitaphs read as personal license plates with limited word space and this is all that is left from family vacations taken year after year in a 1972 AMC Ambassador station wagon. They read like rock candy fading in the mouths of those suffocating children. There is nothing much to say about them anymore. They've dissolved already and their teeth have fallen out.

Happiness

Awards line the walls at *Empire*. "Thanks for participating in…" and "We appreciate your generous donation to…"

Tokens of gratitude and kiss-ass sentiment buying next year's donations for this year's head-ripping club specials. It's called "Bidness" and it lines the walls beneath portraits of the men in the Empire family. Men in plaid and polyester with sculptured hair. Men with airbrushed and blackened eyelining.

Men with money-lined pockets and the smiles and knowledge that money can't buy happiness.

Men. Smiling. Happy. Rich. Men.

Ashtray Collector

Scott had hated ashtrays ever since his sixth birthday, shortly after his grandfather died.

"He would've wanted you to have it," Grandma Pee-Wee mumbled between vodka and orange juice haze that she'd worn as perfume since he'd known her.

Everyone on his mother's side of his family drank. The corner liquor store smelled like a portrait of their yearly family reunions he'd attended stoned as a child.

"What is it?" Scott asked.

"It's your Grandpa's fucking ashtray," she replied. "What the hell does it look like? Take the son of a bitch!"

He did. The first in his ashtray collection.

Every holiday or birthday he would hear his mother on the phone to would-be conventional gift givers, saying. "Oh, Scott would love it. He loves ashtrays. He's a collector, you know?"

Scott hated ashtrays.

Writer

Scott was a man of many faces. He was a car salesman who wasn't at work. He was a cocaine-smoking addict. He was nude. He was one hell of a used furniture salesman. He was a friend. He was a writer. Well, maybe not really a writer.

Scott liked to entertain the idea that he was a writer. He tried to be a writer. He thought he was a writer until the Internal Revenue Service said he wasn't actually a writer and couldn't use his apartment for his office, making it a tax write-off. The IRS didn't think he was a writer. He never asked if they had the qualifications to know such things.

He had been writing for twelve years and, though not yet published, had finally found the book concept that he thought would help him break into the writing business, *The Cow Experiment: All Parts with Exception (Not a Desert Survival Guide for a Runaway Teenager)*.

Yip, this would do it. Unfortunately he had barley finished writing his first draft when the IRS informed him of the bad news. News about him not being an actual writer. He hated hearing this type of news.

His mother phoned him weekly to remind him that he wasn't a writer. He didn't need the government jumping in on her gig. If they were polite enough to wait for her to die (she too should be dying any day since she's old) they could have the job all to themselves. Nope. They wanted to cut in and take over. "You? You're no writer. Are you published?"

The weekly conversation between Scott and his mother was similar. She'd call, "*Ring!*" And he'd answer, "Hello."

"Son?"

"Yes, Ma."

"So you got a real job yet? No more car salesman bullshit. Your stepfather says "hi," and I just wanted to see what you were up to."

"I'm doing fine, Ma. I have a new girlfriend."

"I asked if you had a job."

"She's really sweet. She's Catholic, or something."

"Catholic!" (Silence)

"Ma?"

(Silence)

"He, Ma? You there?"

"Son?"

"Yeah?"

"Catholic, eh?"

"Yeah. I think so."

"Does she have a job?"

"Ma."

"So. You're a writer? How come I can't buy your book in the store? Eh? Answer that, will ya?"

"I'm not published yet, Ma."

"See? I told you. I told your Aunt Vern. You're no writer. You're a plumber like your stepfather. Hey Orvil, tell your kid he's a plumber."

"You're a plumber!"

"See? See? Didn't I tell ya? You're a plumber. Come home and work with your family."

"Ma."

"Come home son."

"Ma."

(sobbing)

"Ma! I'm going now, Ma. Bye."

(Still sobbing) "Son? Come home. Be a plumber. You're no writer."

Click

Remembering the Sex Life of Don & Anne

Don sat up in bed with the newspaper, reading the sports section, mumbling.

Anne rolled her pubic bone in a circle while straddling his thigh. "Honey. Let's screw."

"What?! Nine points? You gotta be kidding. What mastermind allowed them nine points? They're the fuckin' Saints for Christ's sake!"

Track Star

In high school Anne was a track star. She could've easily chased Don down and said things like, "Stay and we can try to work it out!" or "What the fuck do you think you're doing, leaving me with all these bills?"

She didn't.

She waited until he was gone and she stopped crying and began thinking of how she could've caught him if she'd wanted to. She didn't want to. He was gone.

Sitting up in bed with her ankles hanging over the hardwood floor she realized that it was over. No more nights of watching the space where the T.V. used to be, feeling guilty for not saying "Yes." No more warm bursts of gas on her sleeping stomach. No more Don.

The morning sun touched her through the window, lighting her ankles and half-hidden nude body. She sat looking at her ankles with a pillow in her lap, remembering how fast she could run in high school.

Free

Slaves have spoken of the inherent beauty that they first recognized in their own ankles when the shackles were removed. Even the bleeding, scabrous, and scarred ankles are beautiful in the light of dawn, freedom.

Anne stared at her feet that hung over the hardwood floor from her bed. Her legs free from her ivory perfect blinding thighs. She watched her ankles moving free in the morning sunlight.

Scarred.

Beautiful.

Free.

No longer crying.

Throwing and Catching

The bookie comes early to collect. He'd written them down days before and returns to remind us of how easy it is to lose. He returns to remind us of our inability to change destiny. He comes after the quarterback throws.

The quarterback is the second hardest position for a boy to play. He has to dodge and sprint and fold back and drop in and fake short or throw long. He has to stand there with everybody's eyes on the ball. He has to stand there while everybody watches with all their expectations and all their amazement and all their money on the ball. He has to be there to celebrate and be called a hero or a fucking asshole. He has to be asked by reporters why he didn't throw or why he didn't throw well or why he threw at the wrong time, and occasionally how it feels to win.

It's the quarterback's job to throw and amaze us all, carrying our childhood dreams and failures on his victory; high over his head; on his ball. The game ball. The big game ball.

He does his job well and the ball travels toward the end zone. It travels through yards and sky, over defense and offense, spiraling. Up and forward, turning, almost forever. It travels as if forever, turning above everybody, hoping someone will be catching. Hoping someone will be watching. Hoping.

Rust & Steel

I sell more than nuts and bolts and rust and steel. I sell more than cars to people who come to visit me for no reason but to pull open doors and look under hoods or reach into trunks and drive like my grandfather on PCP.

I sell family reunions and Sunday morning picnics.

I sell Friday's big game between cross-town rivals with the offensive line riding behind mom. Throwing sunflower shells and screaming at the top of their lungs in mom's minivan.

I sell nostalgia. I sell emergency rides to emergency rooms. I sell fear. I sell black coat and tie clean dressed teenagers taking the day off to cry about loss. I sell death.

It happens everyday. We have no choice or chance to dismiss this. It happens. Shit, what do we expect? The Earth, like our life, is connected to our death and nothing turns forever. Nothing turns forever. Right?

Right

Nobody catches a big game ball more than once. Nobody.

There are fifteen minutes between each locker room victory party and each broken leg one yard from the end zone. Fifteen minutes from the shower Sunday morning to our breakfast table, where we read the paper with a near-sighted forefinger too fat to ignore while poking ourselves in the eye. "Good job, self! Damn good job."

We catch our own pass and we deserve to smile. Smiling, we can be happy, even if only for fifteen minutes.

As If

He's been smoking since he was fourteen. The cigarette has never gone out and it's a world record. He sold cars once, so he knows this. He knows this and he lies when it's convenient.

His eyes are busy while he drives. Being old and retired now he has some interesting behaviors.

He's deaf, nearly. He squints as if to hear an ant walking across the dashboard. Mumbling quietly to himself, he doesn't allow the voices in his head to answer. He can't hear himself talk.

He tries to read his own lips in the rearview mirror, though this is difficult to do with squinted eyes. Besides, he doesn't believe anything he says to himself; he was a car salesman before he retired.

Maybe she'll stop pissing long enough to answer his questions.

Child

Don tipped his coffee cup, startled at his reflection. No beard on the man in the mug. He had a beard yesterday. It was gone. He shaved it off after three years.

His face looked young. Not as young as it had three years ago before he grew the beard, but younger than it had looked yesterday. Something happened to his face while covered in hair.

This twenty-four-year-old child in his coffee had been a friend of his that he'd been missing lately.

"Hi," he introduced himself to himself again, tipping his cup for a sip of his reflection.

She Should've Known

"What are you doing?"

"Shaving," he said with the tone of an eleventh commandment.

"Yeah. I see that. Why?"

"Can't a man shave?" Don replied, kicking the door closed in Anne's face.

No Click

She should've known he was leaving.

North

"Kat."

"Yeah?" she replied wiping a non-existent spot off the counter top, which is what all waitresses have been trained to do when they're finished bringing toast and coffee and stuff.

"So does this bus go north?"

"You going north?"

"Yeah," Don grinned. "North. If the bus is heading that way."

Kat walked over to the booth where Don was sitting, placing her hands on her hips. Underneath a slight twist of her head and a couple quick smacks of gum, Kat smiled down at Don. "Well, you're in luck, kid. This bus, when it shows, is goin' north."

Some people's heads seem to bounce when they're feeling submissive. Don was feeling this way under the statuesque silhouette that draped Kat. His head bounced like crystal, careful not to break, not knowing what else to do with his hiding eyes and speechless, shadowed mouth.

"Thanks, Kat."

"Sure, kid."

She motioned to return to her side of the cafe. Don lifted his head, looking at her walk away. "Hey, Kat. Sit here with me. Won't you?"

"What?"

"If you don't got much to do, I mean..." Don moved his arm through the room at empty space. "Come on. Have a seat."

"Okay, kid." Kat untied her apron and tossed it behind the counter. She brought a coffee cup with her. After topping off his cup, she poured her own.

"Don," he said over the edge of his cup.

"Don?"

He nodded. "Don's my name."

"Nice name, kid."

"Thanks. I didn't have a choice. My parents named me Don. Kind of the way the world is. When it's time to do something as important as give yourself a name that you'll carry around like baggage all your life, you're fifteen minutes old and have no idea how to let them know what you'd like to be called."

"Come on. Knock off the self pity. Don is a great name."

"A second ago you said 'nice.' Poodles and Boy Scouts are nice."

"You don't think your name is nice?"

"Well, I guess it's nice. Haven't thought of it *that* way, to tell you the truth."

"Really?" she said leaning back in the booth, blowing his name over her cup of hot coffee. "Don…Don…Nice name."

"Thanks, I guess."

Maria's Voice

Some things reminded Scott of smoking. Whenever he sold a car he liked to have a cigarette afterwards. Whenever he wrote he enjoyed a cigarette by his computer. Driving through town at night with his window wide and sixteen-year-old mosquito-breasted blondes beaming at him made him want a cigarette. Then there was Maria's voice.

Maria had a voice that turned all men into Marlboro cowboy advertisements.

Maria spoke with a tongue made of honey and jalapeno. She was a tight-assed, twenty-four-year-old who Scott figured to be a Mexican. Her body can be seen in the back room of every fifty-year-old's mind, dancing in her anal floss undies and giggling polite Spanish phrases. She had an accent when she felt it would benefit her.

Maria's voice reminded Scott of sex, and sex reminded Scott of smoking. When Maria spoke Scott smoked. She didn't mind. Their conversations were almost always by phone and the phone calls didn't come very frequently.

The phone had been ringing. He couldn't answer it.

Ashtray II

He wished he could answer the phone. He'd like that almost as much as smoking his cocaine. The phone continued to ring.

Ring!

Maybe he'd answer, "Hello."

"Hey, Scott. This is Maria."

"Hello, Baby. What's up?"

"Not much. Got a question for you."

"Shoot" he'd say, running his finger over the edge of his birthday ashtray, wishing he had a cigarette for the telephone conversation. He'd like to smoke while on the phone with Maria.

Maria would talk while he would make a few polite, reflecting statements like, "Oh." and "Uh-huh." while continuing to rub his ashtray.

I don't talk with Maria on the phone much, he'd thought. That cigarette sounds pretty tasty.

"Are you listening to me?" Maria always questioned in her sexiest Mexican accent.

"Yeah," he always said, not listening, "I hear you. Go on."

She Should've Known

The first time Anne saw Don he was between her and the lowfat chutney yogurt. He was standing in a group of nursing students with a collective IQ less than their average breast size. He'd been sharing his theory on deep-tissue massage with them while Anne was attempting to find her way around them.

Don and Anne were in each other's eyes for a moment. Not a short moment. An eternity. A moment long enough to assure that they'd find their way back to each other in the near future.

Anne remembered this on their first date. "You'd look great with a beard!" She hated beards.

"A beard?" Don replied. Though he'd never before grown one, he hated beards as well.

"Your face is a perfect beard face," she said. You'd look like an idiot and no little blonde nursing students would dare have any interest in you, Anne thought.

No little blonde nursing student would touch me, Don thought.

That night Anne fucked him and he grew a beard. It was a relationship now.

She should've known he was leaving.
"What are you doing?"
"Shaving!"
"Why are you leaving?"

"I want little blonde nursing students to follow me around in heat." Don kicked the door closed in Anne's face.

No Click

Yep. She should've known he was leaving her when she saw him standing between her and the lowfat chutney yogurt.

New Bed

"Let's buy a new bed!" Anne had read that people tend to associate their bed with whatever quarrels might have taken place in them. In the latest *Cosmo* article it suggested that in order to help improve a couple's sex life after having such bad luck in their bed they buy a new one.

"Okay." In the latest issue of *T.V. Guide* Don had read about a couple that attempted to make foolish, last-minute major purchases in an effort to validate their marriage. They ended up divorcing and going bankrupt. "Let's put it on your Visa!"

They bought a hand-carved bed shaped like a giant clam shell. It was a virgin bed and remained that way for the four-month period that preceded their break-up.

Blue

"Blue."

"What?"

"Blue. Your eyes are blue," Kat smirked, drawing herself through the comfort of her coffee. "I don't believe I've ever seen eyes as blue as yours."

"What? Sure you have. Blue is blue," he replied.

She shook her head.

"What do you mean? Blue is blue. What else could blue be?"

"This guy I knew, David, his eyes were blue. And Matthew had the brightest eyes I've seen. His eyes were teal though. Oh, and my sister Mary. She dated an angel whose eyes were the fairest color of the sky. But you? Don. Your eyes are blue and nobody has eyes as blue as yours."

"Eyes are eyes. I don't even like my eyes."

"Kid, anyone with eyes as blue as yours has reason to love them."

"My eyes remind me of my mother's eyes. I don't like my mother or the eyes she gave me. I haven't seen her in over a year. She never calls or comes to visit."

Kat shook her head, looking out the window beside them. "Take it from someone who hasn't seen her mother since her thirteenth birthday. I'm sure it must have been difficult for my mother to keep me. There had to be some pressure she was under. Something. Some good reason."

Don sat as motionless as an iguana in peanut butter and listened to Kats' story. "Where's she at?"

"You ever wonder what she looks like now?"

"Wonder? Yeah, I wonder." Kat turned to look at him. "Every day I wonder. I work here, behind this counter, and see strangers coming and going every day. I see them come in and I talk to them and I look at them and say to myself, 'Does she look anything like you?' Every day I watch when the buses drive up and the little old ladies file off and come inside to use the restroom or order coffee. I watch them and I think, could she be my mother?"

Kat turned her face to the window, crying those tears that have no sound. Just tears. "I wonder, every day."

Twenty Bucks

The problem with consumers these days happens to be that they feel a car salesman would fuck their dead aunt for a twenty.

Coins

We stand around and talk about the latest deal, or the strangest deal that happened this week. We stand for no reason but to look like salesman waiting for a dollar to fall from the air and we watch the freeway go by. We watch the freeway go by and occasionally we throw a quarter against the sidewall of a tire.

Income is income. The coins are worthless unless they're collected in one of our pockets.

Mr. Empire will fire anyone for grab-assing. He's barley alive, crisp from bourbon and red-skinned, pickled to perfection. The best car man stolen money could buy.

I once said that the day he dies I'd piss on his grave. He came up to me that afternoon to remind me that I would have to wait in line. I told him it would be my pleasure.

Communication Problem

Scott sold a truck last week to a man who stood outside his own house and waited an hour and a half until his wife would let him come in. Fifteen minutes is an eternity. We're talking six times an eternity.

He stood for more than an eternity outside his own house, 11:00 p.m. and sixteen years into a marriage about to end because Scott sold him a truck. She didn't like trucks. Trucks weren't her first choice of things to buy today. Things like food and electricity. He had no idea.

They'd been married for sixteen years and he never learned Korean. She never learned English. They had a communication problem. He bought a truck. She hated his decision. They had a communication problem before Scott sold him his new truck. She doesn't like trucks. He never knew.

Curtains

She made the curtains herself. She was handy as a seamstress.

Long before his retirement she had found her favorite dress. It was a dress she'd sewn for her high school prom and it hadn't fit her in twenty years. It hadn't fit her when she tossed it into a cardboard box and placed it under her father's bed. Her father died and she cleaned his room, finding her favorite dress.

She can sit on the toilet while he drives, and stare out the window between the new curtains she made from her old life. They're the best curtains she's ever seen and they toss in the freeway breeze just enough for her to see outside.

Maria's Phone Call

The phone rang while Scott traced his memory for his grandfather's ashtray. Maria still spoke in the background; he gave little attention to this.

He had his first cigarette when he was six. It was one he had found in his grandfather's closet and he kept it with his ashtray. He used to walk around the house pretending to be a smoker, mimicking the great dead smokers of his lifetime: John Houston, Salvador Dali, John Wayne, etc. His parents thought he was cute.

"Adorable. Look at him. Just like Uncle Jim."

"Cute."

It wasn't until Scott turned nine and began to experience his playing-with-matches stage in life that he had a means or entertained the idea of lighting his cigarette.

Your typical hazy, drizzling, worthless, "where's the Sun?" type of day surrounded Scott and a freshly lit pile of leaves he'd drawn together to burn. He watched it, with his hands shoved in the side of his overalls, elbows bent, chest out, proud.

His cigarette, which he'd carried for the last three years in an old cigarette box, seemed to announce itself. It fell from his overall pocket into a puddle of dried mud at his feet. Picking it up, looking at the fire, he knew it was time.

Cigarette smoking wasn't all it was made out to be. He coughed, turned purple-ish, and his stomach flipped upside down. Then, "*BLRRP!*" he barfed. He would've quit smoking at that very instant if he hadn't already had the habit of using the cigarette as a prop in his every-day, nine-year-old life.

He was an official smoker, carrying cigarettes wherever he went. Since he didn't like the vomiting side effect he wouldn't always light his cigarette. He'd walk around, swaying it in one hand and talking like the Duke, "Well, Pilgrim, You wanta smoke? You gotta know how to barf."

With the onslaught of higher education, Scott became a real smoker in one day. A few children teased him for not lighting his smoke. He was forced to do so or get beaten up. He couldn't throw away the cigarettes because his parents thought it was very cute and he didn't want to disappoint them. His only choice was to light it, which is exactly what he did, and all the kids said, "Ahhhh!" amazed that he lit it, and he became a smoker. "Scott the Smoker."

Now he's in his twenties, enjoying the smoker's life: coughing and spitting phlegm and showering friends with bad breath. He hasn't been able to smoke in eight days and Maria is calling on the phone.

Somewhere up in the Mountains

Scott's mother hasn't washed her hair in a week. The shirt she's pulling out of the dryer, she'd placed there fifteen minutes earlier. She took it from the floor where she'd dropped it the night before.

It's cold where she lives, somewhere up in the mountains, a tiny redneck area. No crosses burn on her lawn. She doesn't have a lawn.

He'd Lost

Scott grew up in the same neighborhood, somewhere up in the mountains. His neighbors smiled through a collection of tobacco stains while roaming the streets. There were fifteen jobs and two thousand, two hundred and four residents. Nobody had anywhere to be.

"How de do?"

"Howdy."

"Hello."

"Good day, folks."

"Well darn, Marlon. How da hell ya been?"

"Jake! Hey, hey, hey…"

"Howdy, dear."

"Well, hello!"

Who knows what really happened to his best friend. Maybe he died and that is all. Maybe the town folks bored him to death. Maybe he went swimming at the crik, ran into his cousin, had anal sex with her and never came back. Maybe he drowned? Ran away? Maybe. Maybe not. All he knows is there is no one to play checkers with anymore. He hasn't played since seventh grade.

He Lost to No One

He sat down beside the checkerboard. These are the same pieces he used to play with during grade school. They were pieces his grandfather had carved from the fig tree beside his front porch. Barely any color remained to differentiate the black from the red. None of this mattered; his friend was dead. There's no way a dead friend can play checkers. He moved the pieces alone, thinking like his friend would've, and lost to no one.

Musician

Anne played the flute before she met Don.

She was incredible. She'd sit on her bed and she'd play with her window half-open. Neighbors would clap when she was finished. Sometimes they'd scream out requests for her to play. She would've played their requests if it weren't for the fact that she only knew one song. She was incredible at it.

This was before she met Don. Before they went out on a date and they fucked and he grew a beard. Before they had a relationship, when she could play her song on the flute, incredibly.

Don hated the flute. "Stop playing that fucken thing!"

She stopped playing it and put it away in a box under the bed that they didn't have sex on.

Tears

It's strange how most tears are accompanied by loud bursts of noise. Occasionally, someone will just simply cry. They cry and you know they're feeling bad, but there isn't any sound. It's a 1922 silent movie that they're crying and you have to sit there in your seat, reading the captions, crying out loud for them.

Mothballs

Four pairs of pants, seven-hundred socks, a pocket full of change, and a box of mothballs helped hide her flute under the bed that they didn't have sex on.

"A quarter," Anne said while lying on the floor, her nude body warming in a haze from the window, and stretching like a fish in the sunlight, trying to reach her flute. It was too far away from her for her to reach. Three years out of reach.

Twenty Long Fucking Years

She's been with him for twenty years. Since she turned 22, he's been seeing her. He was thirty then and she knew he wouldn't live much longer. It was perfect until she went and fell in love with him. Now she would hate it if he died. It would change her whole life; she'd need to find someone else to fall in love with, to smoke with, to laugh and drive and retire with.

She'd need to do a lot of things if he fell over dead right now. Things not to important, like taking out the trash herself, and very important things like getting off the toilet and steering the RV to a safe stop.

They've been together for twenty years. She wouldn't want him to go and die now. It wouldn't help the situation.

Nicotine & Eggs

Scott used to have a cigarette for breakfast. No eggs. No bacon. No cereal or toast. Nope. Just a cigarette and he was pleased, ready to roll the day and take it's pocket money.

Today would be like the last eight days have been, different.

The first day Scott tried jogging to forget he wanted to smoke. He lost his breath at the bottom of the stairs that lead to his apartment. He took a nap outside. No, jogging wouldn't keep his mind off smoking.

Cocaine worked for a few days. He never thought of smoking. He was busy worrying about whether his heart would explode through his shirt and litter his empty living room. Cocaine was the cure until it reminded him of death.

Anytime "death" is mentioned, Scott feels like smoking. This happened to be one of those times.

Scott swore off exercise. "No more exercise!" he said. "Where's my cocaine?"

It's easier to sleep through the morning hours and not have to think about breakfast, which would keep Scott from thinking about his breakfast cigarette. He'll sleep the next few days.

He would've slept today but the phone rang, *"Ring!"* and he was up. Simple as that. From sleep to his Maria calling. Yep, Scott deserved a cigarette.

Hunter

It's important for a car dealer's windows to be clean. When you sell cars this close to the desert vultures slam into your windows every day. It's important to clean the blood and vulture crap off the windows before the customers arrive.

There's this guy who washes windows in the morning. He has no one that he loves, and no reason to sleep. He'd rather clean windows and recall the time he became a hunter, early in his adolescence. One day he was picking his nose and eating candy-coated apples, then *"Blam!"* he was crazy. He was a man. Beyond pubic hair, pimples, and nocturnal emissions, he became a hunter.

Now he washes windows for a living. He washes windows and smiles, thinking about vultures dying and recalls how he is a hunter. He's a hunter and he daydreams of blood running down a mountainside like a rubber squeegee melting in Arizona. He does this with a smile and he does this all for minimum wage and nobody loves him. He's a martyr, too.

Three Years

"Got it!" she exclaimed to her empty bedroom as if it had been rooting for her, which it had been doing for the last three years.

The Phone

Ring

Kat had stopped crying her silent tears and walked over to the counter to answer the phone. She leant down to pick up her apron and wiped her face.

Ring

Scott listened to the phone ring, wishing he could answer it, wishing he had a cigarette or some cocaine or some oxygen.

Ring

"All right! All right, already. I'm coming," she said to a telephone that in no way could've heard her because it's an inanimate object and these type of objects aren't capable of hearing

Ring

"Hello. Dolly's."
Don watched.
"Hello?"
(Dial tone)
Click
"Assholes!"

Spit

Flutes seem to have a peculiar taste to them after they've been stored under a bed where no sex has been performed. Anne's flute had that taste.

She pulled it out of its cherry wood box, where it rested in a miniature blue, crushed velvet casket. Its surface was still as warm as she remembered it being the last time she played her song before she put it away, *Click*, and slid it under the bed. It was a beautiful song and she hoped she hadn't forgotten how to play it.

Anne always played with her window half-open. She liked the warm currents from the street outside. They'd tickle her nose with the exhaust and curl her toes in the fresh sunlight that only came through half-opened windows in November.

She opened her window halfway.

Raising the flute to her mouth Anne craned her neck like all flautists have been trained to do to look as adorable as possible while they play. Her fingers clicked the keyholes to assure they were awake.

Three years is a long time and flutes have been known to hibernate for periods of time as long as that. Her flute was awake. It hadn't slept. It had been waiting for her to play her song again.

She blew and spit showered her half-opened window that she was standing behind.

Pringff dddaringkff

It was appalling. She knew where to place her hands. She knew how to look adorable playing. She knew how her song should have sounded, though it wasn't obvious by the noise she produced.

People need to be fine tuned now and then. Three years of no sex and Anne and her flute needed a few adjustments. Still, looking as adorable as ever, she played her song and thought it was beautiful, again.

Pringff dddaringkff
(Spit)
da de pringff...

She's Tired of Wiping

She expected the RV to swerve at some point but he hasn't died yet.
He's still smoking his retirement cigarette and she's nearly finished pissing and looking out the window. It's early in the day and there is little
death this early to be taken for granted.

That's fine. A man saw her pass as she wiped herself. She saw him see
her as well. It's all right because the gas station is still a few blocks away,
her husband isn't dead yet, and she has a restroom on board.

She'll let people look at her sometimes when she's on the toilet. It
turns her on.

Last

The veterans stand shyly and smirk. They stand, smirking, listening to the green-peas talk wild-eyed and smacking gum, smoking cigarettes through ten buck sunglasses and two buck egos. They stand and smirk and recall when they were just as new, believing that they were invincible; believing that all the chalk on the unit board was as equal to rungs on a ladder into heaven or some place just a notch better than hell.

There is little faith in a three-month veteran found still floating behind the eyes of a sales manager. Less faith in the world and its shortcomings than noticeable on any day except the last day of the month.

Last month Scott set a new store record; 20 units and $9700. This month he's made-$120. (One deal from last month unwound. It happens.) Nobody's seen Scott for three days. Maybe he's dead. Maybe he's not. What's amazing is that I forgot about him this morning and nobody even talks about him anymore, wonders where he is, or seems to give a shit. Nobody, but the new guy.

Deal

One week and no sale. Everybody gets their chance. John is being restrained at the Oakdale Rest Facility after an apparent suicide attempt. His wife has called the sales office four times this morning looking for sympathy and an apology from the closer who told him to get a job flipping burgers.

It's been a hard month for everyone. Tomorrow they'll probably fire us all. In the meantime, I need to collect all debts to pay my bills. I spin the key freely, looking over the dashboard. Nobody is smiling and there are no football heroes in front of the showroom. The salesmen stand while their reflections in the newly washed window fall like a tiger on valium. My car spits and sputters with feather-tipped toe on accelerator and smile chipped nicotine stained teeth grinning.

I drive away in my American car. My new, neon green Dodge Shadow, demo. My car is as American as a stoned twelve year old gang member's graffiti death. I am the spray can he uses. My breath writes your name.

Name Change

If he wanted to be a writer he couldn't have a last name like Zimmerman. "Whose gonna buy a book from a Zimmerman?" he thought. "Nobody."

"Books are a compulsive buy," remarked Dr. Leroy Washington, who was a pioneer in the field concerning the psychology of book sales. The Doctor was on all the major talk shows, discussing his theories. Scott made a point to watch them all.

Scott visited the bookstore once a week. He'd walk in and go to the first section that lured him, the fiction section that began just to the right of the "New Releases." He'd close his eyes, stick out his club of a hand, and randomly grab the first book he came in contact with.

"Darwin." He'd read the author's name and return the book to its place on the shelf, taking note of the name to be written down when he returned to his apartment.

"Darwin," he'd write, comparing the name alphabetically to other names he'd gathered in the same fashion.

"Twenty-seven percent of all books purchased are bought by compulsive book-buyers." Dr. Washington had said that nobody goes to the back of the bookstore to compulsively buy a book. They stand in the door and look around. They spot a pretty cover with huge, friendly letters and they buy it. They don't kneel or reach for a book. If they don't spot something like that they browse only to the beginning of the fiction section. They stick their arm out and *"Wham!"* they're a book-buying addict, on their god-forsaken way to Book-Buyers Anonymous.

"My name is Elizabeth and I'm a Book-Buying Bitch."

"Hello, Elizabeth!"

Scott had done his homework. If for some reason a publisher enjoyed one of his manuscripts, he wanted it to have every advantage. It would've been nice to have a book on the shelves, but he wanted to sell the book as well.

A virgin writer probably wouldn't get the advertising budget of someone like Steven King, glossy color layouts in the "New Releases" section. No. He'd have to get as close to that section his own way. Change his name. Something catchy. Something not so Jewish. Something simple and easy to remember. Something like "Rice," or "Steele," but closer to the beginning of the alphabet.

Jingle

Cafe doors usually have bells on them that jingle when they're opened. This door was no exception to the rule.

Jingle

...and somebody entered.

Kat turned to look at the door. There were no silent tears on her face, just footprints they had left, drying under the dim cafe lights. She yelled to the cook, who had been sleeping since he'd arrived to work. "Hey, Max! Wake up. Breakfast rush."

"Gotta phone?" a sixteen year old blonde with huge white teeth promptly said in an effort not to disturb the cook's sleep.

"False alarm, Max! Right there."

It was too late. Max was awake, which is not a good thing for Max to be at 7:52 a.m. "Fuck, girl. It ain't eight! Can't I sleep without this harassment thing?"

Kat stood, hands on hips with her back to Don, peering under the heat lamps into the back corner of the kitchen. "Listen, asshole. There are customers here. Can't you watch your trashy mouth?"

"Watch your trashy mouth," Max mumbled in a sing-song voice, mocking Kat from a place in the kitchen where nobody could see him. It's a place he'd been many times before. Nobody had ever seen him while he was in that place. Maybe nobody had ever looked.

It Didn't Matter

The teenage girl couldn't have heard Max. She was standing with hair so soft that she would've had trouble hearing her own voice, let alone one coming from a cook, deep in a place that nobody had ever seen.

Neighbors

Anne's neighbors used to listen to Anne play her flute and they'd make requests. This time was no different from the others.

"Will you shut that fuckin' noise up?! People are tryin' to sleep!"

She closed her half-opened window.

A Place

Scott is familiar with that place. It's a place cooks might not be seen in. It's a place that feels like coming home after twelve hours work, the last three blocks approaching the driveway. Lights are on. Everyone is asleep. Dinner wrapped in cellophane. He may have been far too tired to kiss anyone goodnight, had they been there when he needed them.

Home sounds like a flute bending its neck through the nighttime horn bursts and lights popping down Vegas back streets and alleys.

Names

Crosby

Scott A. Crosby

Douglas

Scott A. Douglas

Evans

Scott A. Evans

Waiting

She came in to use the phone. She had no use for bacon and eggs, the traditional early morning artery stopper. She had no use for cholesterol, tabasco, cellulite, caffeine, or the dusty smell of an almost empty cafe. The phone was all she was concerned with, which was obvious to note by the way she stood, staring at it.

Teenage girls all wait for the phone to ring in the same manner. Their hands are cupped in a subtle "I think my hands belonged to a member of the Donner Party in a past life" type of still life. They stand, eyes fixed on the phone, like a sculpture of a politically correct pizza delivery person.

Night School

Teenage girls take special night school classes on waiting for phone calls. They read about freezing weather and the effects of such weather on the teenage mind. They take field trips to the North Pole and their final exam is graded on how well they can sit still at their desks with a pencil and a piece of paper, not doing anything but looking every bit sixteen and waiting for the phone to ring.

Ring

She nearly failed *Waiting for the Phone to Ring: 101.*
Tired of waiting, the sixteen-year-old with huge white teeth attempted to stuff her quarter into the phone.

Ring

"Fuck!" She dropped her quarter and it rolled to a place where cooks go and sometimes aren't seen. A place where people claim socks go when they're lost in washing machines throughout America. It rolled to a place where nobody has sex anymore, mixing itself with four pairs of pants, seven-hundred socks, a pocket full of change, a box of mothballs, and an empty space where a cherry wood casket used to lie.

Ring

It was gone forever.

Mothers

Kat returned to the booth where her coffee cup set. "Mothers are hard to come by 'round these parts," she spoke, barely breathing while turning away.

"Sit down."

Kat paused and looked down at him with eyes that would remind you of a children's matinee for the blind. "I gotta get to work. Why should I sit?"

Don tugged at her sleeve, interrupting her, "Sit. Come on."

Kat sat down.

"Donald," he said after a few moments, attempting to break through her glare that had found its way between them.

"What?"

"Donald. That's my name."

Kat smirked, shifting her head in her hands, covering her bottom lip. "Donald, eh?"

"Yep."

"Donald's a nice name."

Flirting, he quipped, "Nice? Boy Scouts and poodles are nice."

"Yes. Poodles are nice," she smiled.

"How long you been working here, Kat?"

"Goin' on ten years. Why?"

"No reason. I was in the eighth grade ten years ago."

"And I'm sure, just as deadly attractive as you are now."

Embarrassed, Don checked the floor.

"You're blushing."

"Well, what do you expect?"

"I'm unsure. Donald, eh?"

"Yep. What were you doing ten years ago? Even better, tell me about the eighth grade for you."

There is this silence that occurs when someone is reminiscing. It's not that type of silent reminiscing that happens in movies. You know, the kind where the air gets all foggy and low nostalgic music starts pouring through the screen? It's not that type of silence.

It's a quiet silence, where nothing moves or changes and there is nothing a person can say that doesn't sound foolish. That was the kind of silence that occurred when Don asked what she was doing in the eighth grade. It was a long silence and Don had wished he hadn't asked.

She had stopped smiling and began fading into an orange checkered linoleum floor with the grace of a barbiturate eagle suicide. She was everything in the room at that very moment. Kat's hair pressed in her tail feathers, draping every inch of her flight through life until she came to rest on that cafe floor, alone. Her giant, orange, checkered linoleum past melted sadly away. Her yesterday went on without Don's blessing. He didn't want it to end.

She turned to look at him. "Katrina."

"What?"

"Katrina. My name is really Katrina. That's what my mother named me. My father wanted Sue. Everyone calls me Kat."

"Katrina," he pronounced her name as if he were carving a thousand-foot feather. "Caw Tree Naa," he said again, pushing his chest out toward her, for her eyes to play with the buttons on his shirt. "Katrina. You have a beautiful name."

She smiled.

He Couldn't Tell His Parents

He couldn't tell his parents he was changing his name. Maybe he could change his name and not tell them and that would be fine. Except, if he didn't tell them then they would have been mad when he published a book and they went to the store to buy it and saw his new name.

"Do ya have any books by Scott Zimmerman? He's my son, the writer, Scott A. Zimmerman."

"No. I'm sorry ma'am. I've never heard of Scott Zimmerman."

"Could ya check the Catholic section?"

"Hmm," the cashier would open the rolodex and thumb through saying, "Zimmerman. Zimmerman. Nope, no Zimmerman's in the Catholic section."

"Ya see, Orvil. I told ya he's no writer."

"Why don't you try this book. It's sensational. It's by a new writer named Scott A. Douglas."

Scott's mother would flip to the back of the book first, which was always what she did. It was her way to see if the book was worth reading. She liked to know what happened on the last page.

Soon she'd begin her frantic motherly screaming, waving her arms like a pelican in heat, fainting and dropping the book, which would remain open at the photo on the back coverlet: a picture of her son the writer, with his new name.

Nope. He wouldn't be able to tell his parents when he published his first book. He'd have to deal with them not knowing he was a published author. This meant that he'd have to deal with his mother's weekly phone calls, whining for him to return home and be a plumber.

There are no plumbers named Douglas. Why couldn't his name have been Douglas to begin with?

Name

Just ahead is a place where I used to go to forget. I'd go there and sit on a curb where I once wrote my name in the wet cement. I'd sit on my name and remember the day I had hair instead of a job. Now I try to remember the streets I grew up on with yesterday's ringlet ghosts of hair rubbing against my neck. The cold air comes in from my window to remind me how long it's been since I found such comfort in that place where my name is.

In the car business they forget your name. You're nobody until you sell something. Nobody until they have a minute to blow sunshine up your ass while you blow them after hours of listening to them yap about how fucking wonderful they are. You blow them and they tell you that you're getting the next promotion with a wink and a nod and smile half witted your direction.

You're perfect for their team and there is no stopping you, the new quarterback. You blow them and you're fucking god.

They love you.

Then they come. They drive to a place where you once grew up. They stand there and they forget your name. You're nobody until you sell a car.

Christmas

Maybe it's Christmas again. The air squeaks and pops around my car driving. I can see others almost already dressed like a fat man in red. They smile, going through the dumpsters, and I use them to find sense in the minutes.

My mother purchased gifts year round to avoid the holiday rush. I still enjoy receiving last years fashions and rejects. It's a Bee-Gee reunion every year, passing like the 8-track tape player I threw through the living room window the year the compact disc player came out.

Donny Osmond sings "Deck the Halls" and I wonder where Christ is.

Pumpkin Pudding

Her flute playing had become as stale as leftover pumpkin pudding on New Year's Eve. She played her song, paying no attention to the faults that ran through the middle, smiling and spitting and hearing her play her song for the first time in three years.

The walls applauded.

It's a Fantasy

Traveling with her and a somewhat irregular bladder many adults have thought of taking their lives. Whenever she went on vacation she took an extra friend along; a friend that nobody would miss if they didn't return. They never returned. Nobody missed them.

Twelve minutes into his retirement and she hasn't come out of the toilet yet.

She's always fantasized about being able to travel and not have to stop for a restroom. The RV was a blessing. She loved it when her fantasy came true. There is little better than pissing at sixty miles an hour.

French Denim

Ring

"Hello?"

Bzzzzzz! (Dial tone)

"Anybody got a quarter?" she asked, not bothering to hunt for the one she'd dropped, knowing it was gone forever. She was mature for her age.

Don was watching her. She stood barely alive with her ass firmly placed in tight name-brand jeans, *"De Giorious,"* or some seemingly French name that meant absolutely nothing except perhaps, "A pair of overpriced jeans."

The quarter was all she had left of her life savings, which she had used to pay for her night school classes and to purchase the pants she was wearing. It was gone forever and there wasn't anything that she could do to change that.

Sixteen

There was something in the way the girl stood, pigeon-toed, lifting her ass in her stonewashed, name-brand jeans that told Don she was sixteen.

"Sixteen," he said to himself.

Kat was leaning against the counter, polishing a non-existent spot on it. For not knowing her mother, she looked as beautiful as a forty-two year old waitress could look. She didn't bother lifting her head to see Don. "Sixteen," she mumbled.

"Sixteen," the cook said, mocking Kat from a spot in the kitchen where he stood out of sight.

Lint

"I think I got some change here," he replied, bending his body to reach the bottom of his pocket. "Let's see." Don withdrew a few marbles and some chewing gum that he'd carried with him since his sixth birthday…

<u>And...</u>

a piece of string that he used to hang Barbie when she learned to speak...

And...

an eight-ball he'd hidden from his childhood friend, Scott, the crack addict...

<u>And...</u>

a condom with an American flag painted on it that he'd bought in the Greyhound station bathroom when he was ten...

<u>Nope</u>

…and a handful of lint.

"Sorry. I was wrong." Don lifted his head to speak to the teenage girl. She had turned away.

Teenage girls seem to have short attention spans and four chapters of waiting for Don to give her a quarter was too much to keep her interest.

She was standing in front of the phone with her butt staring up at him, saying thank you, and bouncing like all teenage girls do. The phone wouldn't ring until she stopped bouncing. She never stopped and it never rang again.

Huge

It might be 6:58 a.m. and time to forget about debt, but you couldn't tell by the way the sun climbs. It rises like blood through cheese cloth. I've seen this only once before in my life, and it's huge. It's as big as the Pope on haldol or being visited by the ghost of Mama Cass.

As far as I knew, none of this has ever happened before. If it had I would've been there instead of pulling up outside Scott's apartment. I would've been the one smiling, looking down at my watch. I would've said something like, "Hmmm. 6:58 a.m. Yep."

More about Scott's Apartment

The walls were nicotine yellow and covered with old photographs of the Nevada Railroad and the Vegas Wasteland. Each photo had a caption and a date that stood out like a nude snapshot of your grandmother at a bar-b-que in 1968.

All his furniture was gone. Sold to feed his crack habit.

All that was left of his family were those photos. Nobody buys old pictures, and pushers are too busy driving needles in veins to drive nails in sheet rock.

The only piece of furniture Scott owned was a box spring and mattress set that he'd spent the last few days pissing and trying to vomit on. He never managed to turn his head to see the phone still ringing. He never managed to reach over and answer it and hear that he was fired. He never managed.

Just Black

Don watched the R.V. pull up outside, drinking his last bit of coffee, wishing he had more.

Coffee is best when it's new, he thought, like love, when you have no idea it's waiting to be sipped. Lips pursed against the walls of the mug and you burn your tongue, beginning the simple cycle of forgetting the taste it left in your mouth. Just black. No cream. No sugar. Just love.

Nipple

The phone hung like a solitary nipple in the center of the farthest wall of the cafe. The sixteen year old girl stood drinking phone-milk, waiting for the phone to ring, and bouncing with hair so soft it couldn't hear her words. She stood there for the rest of her life.

Retirement pulled up outside, it's exhaust breathing Ventura air. She never left the restroom. He had to go inside after pumping the gas to use the toilet.

Doors are strange. They open slowly for those wanting to leave and quickly for those who wish to stay. The cafe door seemed to open slowly as an older lady with bright blue friendly hair followed the retired man inside.

Don stood. "Well, Kat. Time to go."

"Take care, kid."

"You too."

"Max! Breakfast rush!"

Away

Everything has to be put away at some point in its existence. Anne placed her flute back in its miniature casket and pushed it under the bed to the place it had been for the last three years.

6:58 and Beautiful Walking

Anne dressed in clothes she hadn't worn since she first met Don and they fucked and...you know the rest. She wasn't as beautiful as she remembered being before meeting Don, yet she felt like she was. She looked out into the hallway of her apartment building as if she were deciding whether or not to leave her room. She did this after already deciding, but still made the look every part of her routine. We all do this. She did it well before closing the door quickly behind her, *Click*, and walking down the hallway away from her apartment looking beautiful walking.

Fifty

Old for a smoker. No male in his family lived much longer than fifty. They all smoked and ate and died of heart disease. He's retired now, nearly fifteen minutes, and standing in Dolly's with his back to the R.V. that Don is closing the door to.

No Click

He fumbles for a light. The R.V. pulls away and Don smiles while nobody watches, heading north, somewhere in America.

Katrina Would Have Cried

She would've cried but cafe windows are nothing like those found on R.V.s that are leaving.

"Excuse me, honey," an older lady spoke through blue hair with words requiring Katrina's attention. If she hadn't listened to them they would have crumbled away and died before they could've been heard.

"Katrina."

There is something about the Vegas dawn that makes it difficult to hear everything an older lady says while people are driving away from you.

"Yeah?" Kat replied, watching the gases from the R.V. cover it's own steps up the road.

The older lady sat down at the counter and looked over her shoulder at the bus as well. "Cup of coffee, honey?"

Pigeons

Anne rode her elevator to the top of her apartment building. She liked to go up to the roof and sit there with the pigeons. She'd sit on the ledge and stare down at the cars, four stories below. She'd stare and she'd cry while thinking of how big America is.

Ding

Elevators make an obvious *Ding* type of sound when the doors open and close and when they arrive at the floor the person inside requests. Anne looked out the elevator doors at the open air around the building. It swirled like a typical American day. She pushed the button that read *"Tres"* and the doors closed quickly.

Arrival

I knew something was wrong when I saw the dry blood on his cheek and pillow. It was obvious I wasn't going to get the money he owed me. No reason for me to spend much time with him. Dead people don't appreciate visitors as much as nearly dead people do. These are the facts.

I arrived later than I should have and he missed work. He missed work and he missed life. He never woke up for neither. Maybe, if I had arrived last night he might have still been alive. Maybe, if he hadn't been a crack smoking, wannabe writer who steals money from his friends he would have still been alive. Maybe.

After my arrival I left. (We have all done this at one point in our lives.)

Still Life

Anne pounded on his door. He lay inside, dead and late for work.
"Scott! You in there?"
(Dead)
"Hey, If you can hear me, you're late for work!"
(Still dead)
Knock!
(Still)

Genealogy

This had nothing to do with my family or its heritage. I never dreamt of my fathers', father, or what they sold or bought. My mothers' mother spent zero time at the foot of my bed, any closer to the end of the lot where all that steel kept me.

Nobody knows who came from where or what or why they did. Nobody talks about this. I try not to think about it openly anymore. I try not to be seen staring off into her mumbling shadows. I don't hear what I'm thinking. What I do hear has nothing to do with a tree where no family of mine has ever grown.

Looking forward to the future, dreaming and perhaps wondering with some precognition, I slept. I slept watching streets open up beneath me, the river turning under the bridge. I smiled with popcorn fresh in the air; matinee springtime. I ran naked and stoned into the horizon with my mouth wet and ready, wondering. Thinking. The future is here today. It's here and we can see throughout the daylight clearly. We see back toward that one day where we tossed our coins against the wall, tinkle-crunch in still-crisp morning air. The future is here and I now remember exactly what I was looking forward to. I understand.

Conclusion

There is little left to be said. We sadden ourselves by recognizing our similarities in our differences. The lady pissing at sixty miles an hour; the men at the Empire car lot; our mothers, God rest their souls, the dead people and the not so dead people; and those that fit no role in our lives. We're all the same person and we have only one thought.

We're just people and cars. And we move throughout our day. That's all we are. We move looking for some hidden meaning, some thread that binds us, and the answer is simple. We only have to learn that we're making our lives far too complicated. Jesus fucking Christ! We have to learn how to put the two together.

Beginning

Maybe I should've begun at the beginning. It's hard to say now that I've shared everything with you. Everything, that is, except the name of her cat.

Stella.

The white cat who dodges traffic in the morning. The fast, toothless stray that bends its neck to sip coffee with the salesmen. That content feline who coughs up hairballs for dawn like the beginning of a book about cars and people. A good book. One I'll someday write.

> He dreamt at night occasionally of a little chick in a plastic red mini skirt.
> They never met. She was the bitch who placed her whites in the washing machine beside his every Thursday. They only smile at each other and the rest of the time they spend reading magazines trying not to look over the pages at one another, knowing they want to fuck like rabid poodles.
> They kissed only once in his dream. Once, last night. It was the last night they were together.
> *"I think she drives an import."*
> *"He must be a convict."*
> They'll never meet.

End

Car guys scratch and sniff at their posts. They turn around throughout the month and try to get that last up out the door and down the street. They burn out and burn up and die trying to get someone to burn gas. It's the way it's happened for years and the way it will always be. One day it's the middle of the month and everybody is working to make their paycheck and the next day it's the last day.

On the last day your pulse shakes while you look at the chalkboard counting units sold. Eyes comparing worth and worthiness and wide-eyed wondering when they'll get some rest.

Then the night fucks you like you're standing against a streetlamp. One minute you're off and the next you're all lit up and shining on the hood of a strangers' car with a thong around your ears. One minute it's the last day of the month and you need to sell one more car and the next minute it's midnight, December fucking first, and that's all.

It's over. It rolls around on the ground like a cat masturbating. It rolls around on the ground looking inviting until it scratches you. It rolls around in the sunlight of morning, licking its end.

Click!

0-595-25917-0

Printed in the United States
44888LVS00005B/283-291